THE CATS CONFERENCE

Three extraordinary stories of special cats and their adventures.

Follow Jeffrey, Jameson, Bertie, Bob and the rest of the gang as they unlock past life memories and special powers to make a difference to life for the humans and cats in Norman Close and indeed the planet Earth.

By Marian Matthews
Writing as Jasmin Pemberton

Copyright@2025 J Pemberton

All rights reserved. No part of this book may be reproduced in any form without permission from the author.

Jasmin.pemberton123@gmail.com

Cover picture and illustration

By Stephanie Weaver

Additional illustrations by Alex and Jess Bowler and Jasmin (with help from Canva), and Rachael Wallis.

Published by Jaxmax Publishing.

Blandford Forum UK

IBSN 9798283018126

www.marian-matthews.com

Thanks and acknowledgements

I simply could not have taken the leap into fiction and written these cats tales without the support of my husband Toby and my children, especially my daughters Chloe and Emma.

I also thank grandchildren, Alex and Jess Bowler and Rachael Wallis for their illustration contributions. It was them, of course, that gave me the inspiration to turn the stories into a children's book.

The book would also not have been complete without the wonderful illustrations by dear friend Stephanie Weaver. Thank you all.

Contents

The Cat's Conference 11

    1)   An important meeting   11
    2)   The truth about cats   24
    3)   The Close cats   35
    4)   The problem   57
    5)   The solution   64

A very bad kitten 91

    1)   A naughty new arrival   91
    2)   The second conference 102
    3)   Master Bertram   107
    4)   A revelation   117

Bob the intergalactic caravan cat 124

    1)   Imminent danger   124
    2)   Bob's arrival   140
    3)   Protection duty   150
    4)   Rescue   157

SW

THE CATS CONFERENCE

Chapter 1- An important meeting

Driving around the corner of her road on her way home from work Sarah was puzzled. What on earth was going on! What was it that she could she see? It was getting dark, and she was tired. But even so, she was sure that she had seen something strange in front of her car. There in front of her was a small circle of cats. They were standing on the grassy roundabout at the end of her road. This was Norman Close. It was called a Close because it was a dead end. The cats seemed to be doing something strange and spooky! What were they doing, or was she imagining it?

Whose cats were they, and where had they come from? At first glance they looked like the local cats that lived here in her road. She could see a tabby, a couple of sleek dark brownish cats and a smaller black one. There also was a large ginger cat and one white long haired fluffy type. Plus there were a couple of cats who looked like moggies. Moggies are real mixes of cats that could be any breed.

She recognised a couple of them as her neighbours' cats. One cat almost looked like her Silki, who she had left curled up on her bed at home.

Couldn't be though, she thought, Silki would never do something strange like that surely?

In this circle of cats there was no sound, no meowing. A bit of ear twitching perhaps and occasionally a touched paw. There was no doubt that they were talking to each other though. It was very strange anyway. Then suddenly, without warning they scattered into the Close.

It was if they were having a conference she thought. Conferences are special meetings where people get together to talk about problems. They can then come up with plans or ideas to sort the problems out. Then she laughed at herself.

How silly I am, cats do not have conferences or even meetings, she thought. I must have imagined the whole thing.

She drove home and was relieved when Silki met her at the door. Silki twisted herself around her Sarah's legs in welcome.

Ahh there you are, she said, I must have been overtired; the brain can play such tricks. I probably should not have been driving. Now what shall I make for supper?

She had been pleased to be back to her cosy home after her own boring meeting at work. She lived with her much loved and fussed over cat called Silki. This was in a nice comfy house in Norman Close, in Brisport in Somerset.

The countryside began at the end of her road. Beyond the big gate at the end of the road was lovely open farmland with green meadows.

There were trees and lots of wildlife. It was a very peaceful place. At the end of the Close, in front of the gate was the small grassy roundabout that the cats were seen on. This let cars turn around when they could not get any further up the road.

On the roundabout was a patch of scruffy grass and a small quite battered tree. In the middle of it was an old, and now not used, BT telephone relay box. BT or British telecom used to operate all the old fashioned land lines.

This was an oblong grey metal box, about a metre high. Inside were lots and lots of wires. Relay boxes were used before the invention of cable and mobile phones.

You sometimes still see them on the corners of some roads. They made old fashioned landline phones work by connecting lines together.

SW

 This old BT relay box, of course was not all that it seemed to be. It contained a big secret. That secret would prove to be vital in solving a big problem for all those who lived in Norman Close. This would be important both for the cats and humans that lived there.

You may not know that there are miles of invisible tunnels beneath the Earth and beyond into the whole universe. Most humans do not know they are there, although, of course, cats do.

These are called wormholes and are millions of miles long. They connect the worlds in our universe and all through our galaxy. These wormholes are made from special invisible energy material. Most humans cannot usually see them. They work a bit like high speed train tracks. You can go along them at super speed.

People who are able to use them can move quickly between the worlds of our universe. They can even go beyond that. They can travel to anywhere in whole galaxy.

Some of these beings are aliens from other planets. They may not look like people at all. Others are just spirits without physical bodies. Like ghosts really. Not all are the good guys though or even have Earth's best interests at heart.

Like train tracks, the wormhole tunnels have places where they connect with other tunnels. They also have places where beings can go into or leave the tunnels, like stations. These are linked to something called portals. Portals are like invisible magic doors. They can be used to get into wormhole tunnels to travel wherever you want to go.

Or, like at a train station they can be used to come out of the of the wormhole tunnels. You can then enter whatever world you have arrived at.

One of these stations and portals could be found under the old BT relay box on the roundabout. This was not known about by the humans, or even the owners of the box.

The beings that came in and out of the portal used invisibility cloaks so that humans could not see them. The cats of course were quite aware of what was going on but ignored the comings and goings. There was usually a cat that appeared to be sleeping on the box.

They were actually guarding it, not just dozing. They were stopping anything dangerous coming out.

In the end, though it was a problem in the Close that meant the conference had to be called.

23

SW

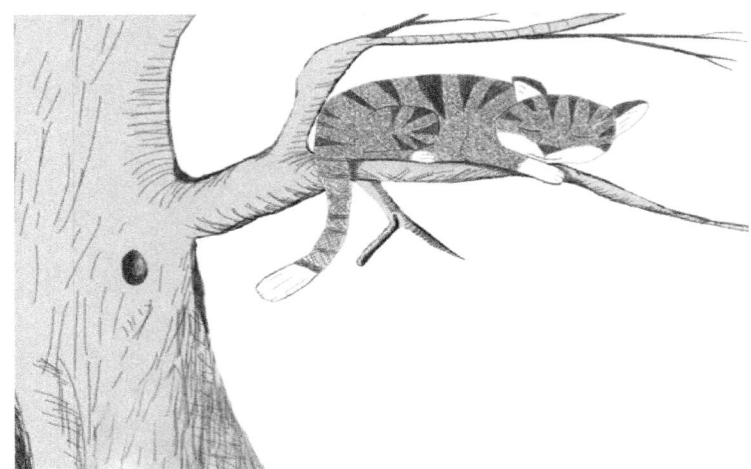

Chapter 2 - The truth about cats

There always seem to be lots of cats about everywhere you look. This was certainly true of Norman Close. At first glance they seem to be simple creatures, cute pets. They seem to be doing nothing all day. Nothing could be further from the truth. Many people make that mistake.

Most humans think that cats have an easy life. Pet cats do not worry about paying bills, going out to work. They never worry where their next bowl of milk, or cat treats, will come from.

Also, their lifestyle seems to involve a lot of sleeping in sunny spots or on sofas or beds. They are said to sleep 16 hours out of the 24 in the day.

Not only that but they can be seen to be roaming about, doing what they like all day. They can be seen playing with other cats and the odd mouse. They look like they do not have a care in the world.

From the catty point of view their humans are seen not as their owners. They are seen as some sort of useful servants. They may be fond of them of course. They have also learnt that showing affection will mean better food or comfort generally.

Some cats even allow their owners to groom them. Grooming is combing their hair and making them look smart. Some owners enjoy this and give the cats more treats.

Cats have learnt that a carefully timed purr, or even a growl can work wonders in training their humans!

Some cats do work for humans. Farm cats work hard killing rats and keeping small animals on the farm safe. Other cats help and protect witches. Witches work at magic and casting spells. Witches always had their black cats to guard and look after them and help with the magic.

These types of cats are not really pets. The Close cats were pets though. They were very well looked after.

This is not the whole story though. Some cats, in their own way, work very hard on levels not seen by most humans. They are doing things that humans cannot see.

For instance, when they look like they are sleeping, cats are sometimes patrolling the wormhole tunnels.

This is not always in cat form. This is done with the power their minds, or spirit. The cat's body looks as if it is still napping. Another copy of themselves is doing the important work.

Cats do have a magical ability to be in two places at once. A spirit body, a bit like a ghost version of themselves appear in the tunnels.

They can change this spirit body into any shape they like. They can become large and fierce, or they can become small and invisible. Then they can get rid of any stray beings from other planets heading for Earth.

This is particularly important for those bad beings who intend to cause damage or harm to Earth. It is like chasing and catching the mice in their owners' homes. This is a vital job to keep the Close and the world safe.

It has to be said that this is not true in every case. Some cats choose to be just cats. They are pets with not a thought in their heads about helping others. This is unless it benefits them directly.

Some of the Close cats were just pets. Although most of them did do the special work. Generally, cats do protect their owners from low level harm, in their best interests of a comfy home, of course.

Just noticing the everyday life of cats, many humans, especially those very busy and stressed, deeply envy their lifestyle. How often have you heard people say that they would love to come back as a cat in their next life.

When you die as human you do not vanish completely. Your body might crumble. But the part of you, called your spirit, will go on to somewhere else. After a suitable time, your spirit may come back into another body and become a human being again. Or you may come back as some other animal, like a cat. You are not supposed to remember any past lives. The idea is you start again each life.

Believe me though the people that always fancied being a cat, always have a shock when that does happen.

The next question is, do people remember their past human life when they come back as cats? The idea is that you don't. You are supposed to come in with what is called a blank slate. You do not remember anything about your past life.

In practice though, this does not always happen. There can be what is called bleed through. That means that you can have some memories of your old lives.

This happens if you have been sent back to Earth for a special purpose. You may be sent back to learn a lesson, to help someone, or as a punishment.

Cats are never close friends with other cats. They are very territorial. That means they claim a territory around or inside their home. They don't like it if other cats come into it and might even fight them. This may happen, even if they share the same house.

The exception to this sometimes is if they are blood relatives. This means mums or dads or brothers and sisters, or maybe even cousins. Even then they do not always get on or even be nice to one another.

RW

Chapter 3 – the Close Cats

Who were these cats who lived in Norman Close and played such an important role in keeping it safe?

The most important cat in the Close at this time was Jeffrey. It was he who spent the most time on top of the old BT relay box, guarding the portal. He appeared to be an old, battered ginger cat with one eye as he strolled around. This was not the whole story about him though.

Jeffrey had been ferocious when he was younger and fitter. He used to strut about his old neighbourhood. Other cats that wanted to take over his old territory were frightened away.

He used to be a very handsome cat. Local boy cats were a bit scared of him. Lady cats admired him. He had been known to scare small dogs with his fierce hissing and hard stares.

Unfortunately, he had had a terrible accident before coming to live at the Close. He could never work out how he came to be living there. The new family seemed nice enough, pesky children of course. Food was reasonable, basket comfortable. But whatever happened to his kindly owner old Bill, who had cossetted him so well over the years?

All he could remember was an awful noise as a car screeched towards him. There was shouting and then darkness. Someone picked him up and took him in a car to a strange place called the vets. Everything hurt. Where was

Bill? Where was his home? Where was his old territory?

After all the operations, and recovery, he had been sent home. But not to home home but to a strange house somewhere he did not recognize.

He spent a lot of time sitting on top of the old BT relay box on the patch of green guarding the portal. He knew what he was supposed to do.

Never a country cat he nevertheless appeared to find peace looking over these green fields. He quite liked his new territory.

Jeffrey, being a practical cat made the best of it. He had, quite understandably, begun to hate cars. Although once he had been fascinated by them.

Unfortunately, next door to the man who seemed to be his new owner, was a man who hated cats but loved cars.

The period of time forever known, throughout the neighbourhood as the Jeffrey wars began. The irony was that Jeffery had of, course, for many years been a racing driver.

Of course he could not really remember it. He had driven a

wonderful fast red car. He had then come to an unfortunate end in a bad crash. But up until the end the thrills had been worth it.

Jeffrey had discovered the soft top of his neighbour's old car. It made a wonderful napping place. It was out of the wind and rain, and perfect for his aching bones. Cat hairs, claw marks and muddy paw prints were always found on the soft top of the car. This always seemed to happen just after the car had been cleaned. Shouts of that darned cat, or I do not believe it, were often heard through the neighbourhood.

Nothing put off determined Jeffrey. Not cat scarers, super soakers or just shouting. He was one tough dude. He became the unofficial chief cat of the Close. They all looked up to him and even were a little afraid of him. As it happened his car sabotage skills were much needed when the problem in the Close began.

Just down the road were two more cats. Their owner was Jill. She lived in a nice house in the Close. Twin kittens had been given to her by a family friend. They were sleek, mostly dark brown cats. They were strange looking even for a mixed breed. At a glance they looked black. It was only close up that you could see their special markings. They did have classical fancy cat faces though. It was almost as if they had stray Persian cat in them. They were named Brandy and Snap. The cats who had been given these names did not know whether to enjoy the joke or be furious at this insult.

They did have some memories of their past human lives. They knew that they had definitely come down in the world! These names were not suitable!

Jill had been lonely when the children left, of course, which is why she had got the kittens. Once the pesky kittenhood was over, much to the relief of all parties, they did provide company of sorts.

The trouble only started when another set of twins, her surly almost grown up sons, came back from university. They were doing media studies. They were called Bill and Ben.

Brandy and Snap did vaguely remember having lives as Egyptian princes, or nobility at least. Amhop and Parsayus were their names in their last physical human life. Brandy and Snap now seemed, to them, totally inappropriate. Truth be told they had not behaved terribly well when human. They had used their twinhood and status to tease and torture their poor attendants and servants. Their own parents had shuddered at hearing their names.

They came, of course, to sticky ends when someone had actually picked up the courage to poison them. They never knew who, although they had their suspicions.

They were mightily miffed when no one seemed to miss them. Their deaths were put down to bad drains, undercooked meat or something similar. Nobody seemed to care.

As cats they did quite miss the status, the weather, and the available servants. After they died there had not been much of a decent burial temple or pyramid built to honour them. This was what usually happened to Egyptian princes.

Also, nothing nice was left with their bodies to ease their way into the field of dreams. This was the Egyptian gateway to a pleasant afterlife. There were no decent grave goods. The nice things like jewels and weapons, that princes are usually buried with, were not put in their tombs. Nobody even cried.

But anyway, given the way they behaved they would not have survived something called the weighing of the soul. This happened just after you died in ancient Egypt. This was done to see if your good deeds in life weighed more than your bad deeds. Their bad deeds weighed way more than their good deeds. In fact no one could find any good deeds! They were lucky not to have been thrown into the eternal darkness. Or perhaps they had. Or perhaps this cat life was another chance for them.

But why Jill, and why cats, they asked themselves, what were we thinking? Their only consolation was to tease and torture Bill and Ben. Subtly done of course, so Jill did not notice. Bill and Ben of course did exactly the same to them. They all rather enjoyed it.

The knack of it all, though, is that you never do remember what you were thinking. That is not the point of it at all. One of the interesting things is though, in a new life you usually don't come back to any one you knew from previous lives. The idea is to experience something completely different. Or to do a particular task that needed doing, of course.

There were other conference cats in the Close. Most of the conference members lived there as it happens. A beautiful but spoilt white long-haired cat called Patrica, lived at number 23. Having long white hair meant lots of grooming. Lots of combing and untangling. Mrs Maxwell her owner was fussy, and she was not really allowed out in the Close much. The compensation for this shut in life was lots of treats. This suited Patricia, although the downside was that she was rather bored. She had also put on an unflattering amount of weight.

Luckily, she had no memory of being an important stressed and busy politician in her last life. Used to having to make hard decisions, she was one of the people who had definitely wanted to come back as a cat. Obviously, she had not quite understood the whole deal though.

She had also not realised how her old skills would someday be very important. That is if she could overcome the brain rot her pampered life was beginning to cause.

As for Sarah's Silki, well, she was someone who had found life very hard when she was human. In her old life she lived in a small damp cottage, which always seemed to be cold. As the eldest daughter she was always having to look after her many brothers and sisters. She was another one who had always fancied being a cat.

As Emma she had always envied the farm mouser. When he was not actually mousing, he always seemed to sleep in the sun or in cosy corners. He as a working cat was always well fed when she was hungry.

As Silki, she initially enjoyed the care provided to her by her owner Sarah. Truth to tell though, it was also beginning to become tiresome and boring. Luckily the events which were going to happen in the Close would change all that very soon.

There was also an unknown number of motley mixed mums and kittens at the relatively messy bungalow at 44. These were of all shapes and sizes. Not all had been previously human. Some were just always cats. There was an odd bear and a python and a possible wolf, but that was all.

They all lived in happy chaos.

A B

 There was young tabby called Simba. In his youth Jeffery would have taken him on in any cat fight for territory and won. As an older and more sensible cat, he kept well clear. Simba was the best and strongest of the young cats living locally. As a tiger striped tabby, he was fit, handsome and full of himself. He was daddy to many of number 44's kittens. Indeed, he was now forbidden to go there. He was not allowed in the house or garden. He usually managed it he wanted to though.

In his last life he was a brave soldier, in fact he was a commando. He still had the energy and bravery although he had no memory of that life.

The twins also kept clear of him. They told themselves that common tabbies were beneath their notice. They were forgetting, of course, their own mixed moggie vintage, as cats and not princes.

JB

There was also another important cat. He was not in the Close all the time. He came and went when he wanted to. He generally did not interfere with the other cats' lives but would assist if there was an issue. Jameson was his name. He was an extra large good looking ginger whiskey coloured cat. He had huge yellow eyes that could be quite scary if they glared at you. He had lots of long wispy hair around his face. This almost made him look just like a miniature lion. He was brave like a lion but was a calm, peaceful and respectful cat. He did not challenge Jeffrey but worked with him to solve problems if needed.

These were not the only cats in the Close, but they were the important ones for our story.

The Close cats happily ignored each other, whilst being very aware of each other's existence. Until, of course, that fateful day, when everything changed.

JP

Chapter 4 - The problem

Most of the cats were a bit slow to notice when the problem first showed itself. Human doings, unless they personally inconvenience them, are generally beneath their notice.

It did gradually dawn on the cats that something was up with their human hosts though. The humans began to all seem very upset about something. The cats had no idea what that was. Cats could not understand human speech. They were forced to try and tune in to their humans' thoughts, as cats can do if they chose. This was called telepathy, it was all terribly inconvenient. Standard of care were slipping.

The trouble seemed to start when a big notice board appeared at the end of the Close. There were pictures of large colourful buildings on it. It also showed lots of little houses and roads. The upset seemed to get worse when important looking envelopes fell through all the letter boxes in the Close.

As far as the cats could generally make out from their owners' thoughts, the notice board meant something bad. It was saying that there was going to be something called a big new housing estate built. This was going to be on the fields behind the Close. This meant new houses and roads. The letters were telling the cat's owners what was going to happen.

This would be a disaster for everyone. The new houses that the builders wanted to build on the fields was bad enough. The worst of it was though that the Close would no longer be a Close.

They were going to take away the roundabout (and portal) and make a new road through to the new estate. Instead of a quiet Close it would be a busy road, with lots of traffic. This would be noisy and dangerous for humans and cats.

The humans got together to talk about things. Their meeting was not useful. They did not know what to do. They had no idea how it could be stopped. A lot of arguments seemed to be going on. They could not come to any decisions.

They did find out that the builders needed something called planning permission from the local council. If they got that then the builders could just go ahead and build. No amount of complaining could stop them.

It was, the cats realised, time for action. This was a problem that they could not trust their, probably ineffective, humans with. Their peace and quiet would be spoilt. Even worse, the extra traffic would also be dangerous for unwary kittens or strolling cats. Jeffrey was particularly firm on this one, having had experience of dangerous drivers before.

It would also be very stressful and noisy while the house building took place. There would also be lots of drilling and hammering. Cars and vans would be everywhere.

There would also be the loss of the field mouse hunting grounds. The most important thing was though, what would become of the portal?

It was time for the cats, under Jeffrey's supervision, to call their own meeting. They would have to, against their basic independent instincts, put their heads together and co-operate with each other on this one.

They met on the grass on the roundabout as it was getting dark, to discuss things. This was the conference that Sarah had seen. The fight back had begun.

JP

Chapter 5- The solution

The first important question of the conference was, how can we, as small cats stop this dreadful thing happening? The answer came quite quickly. As just individual cats they could not do anything much. But what they did have, if they chose to use it, was each other and perhaps find some other help.

Firstly, cats, if they could be bothered, understood the ways things worked in the universe better than the humans. Some of them, at least, knew they had lived lives as humans before. The more advanced cats understood that they could work together.

Harnessing the power of all their minds they may be able to combine their thoughts and access memories from their past lives. They could then use skills developed in past lives as humans. This is an intense process but possible. This was the first task of the conference.

Jameson was particularly helpful here. He had done it before in another neighbourhood. On his instructions they touched paws, said a short spell, concentrated and drew down their past life energies. Then that unlocked the memories and skills they needed to try and solve the problem.

Secondly, they did after all have access to the beings from the wormholes that used the portal. The humans did not know about this, so could not use them. This may take some individual negotiation but was very possible. Some were good guys, some were not so good, they could probably use both.

Thirdly, they were after all, just cats. No one would take any notice of a cat wandering about. They could spy or distract or disrupt very easily.

The important problem to be solved was, how stop the development and to protect the portal. A campaign of individual warfare on the builders was a start.

If they could make it too difficult for the builders to start it would help. They may at least delay things which would give them time to think of a final solution.

For now they would keep it to the Close cats. It would be difficult enough to persuade the Close cats to work together. More cats would be impossible to manage. They may have to call in more help in the future.

The Close cats, following Jamesons advice, agreed that someone should take overall charge. As he was not actually a full time Close cat, Jameson felt it better if someone else did it. Jeffrey did not feel it was his thing. He felt too old to take it on. Who would be best to do it?

Having suddenly got access to her past life, Patricia was jolted into action and volunteered. She was momentarily ashamed of her spoilt life and weight gain. As Lady Harrison she had been a deputy prime minister. She was used to solving major problems, after all.

It was important to conceal their plans from the humans for now. The humans would not have believed what was going on with their pets anyway. In practice it was almost impossible to cover up the changes in the cat's mentality. They were now cat/human hybrids and very tiring it was too.

There was a lot of puzzlement from the individual humans about changes in their pet's behaviour. Luckily, they did not all compare notes and wonder what was going on.

Mrs Maxwell did notice and was puzzled by Patricia's sudden reluctance to eat treats. She had a spring in her step, and a new insistence on going out into the Close. Mrs Maxwell did not actually like it. It was like having a different cat.

The big advantage in all this was that the cats could actually understand exactly what the humans were saying. It was easier than just understanding telepathically what they were thinking.

This was a two pronged campaign. They had to work out what the humans could do and what they could do themselves.

First, as a politician Patricia knew what was the best way was to stop the new housing estate. This was to stop the builders getting permission to build it. Once the builders had something called "planning permission" from the council, that would be that. They could not be stopped from building. No amount of complaining would matter. How could they prevent this happening?

Patricia knew of one way this could be done. This was to do with the environment. Some wild animals and plants are protected by the government. These are called endangered species. There were laws saying that if any of the special animals or plants that the government were trying to protect were living there, the builders were not allowed to disturb them. They would not get the permission from the council to build the houses and roads. Animals like bats, badgers or dormice came into this category.

The next task was for the cats to put certain thoughts into their humans' heads. This was that they should ask the council to do an environmental survey. This is to check that no important wild animals or plants were living there. This would hold things up nicely.

If the cat owners noticed their cats staring at them intensely for long periods of time they did not say anything. The cats were telepathically trying to put the idea of asking for an environmental survey in their heads.

This succeeded, and at the next council planning meeting, all of them asked for one to be done. This was considered clever not strange.

The council, who had not been that keen on the development and did not really want all the houses there, jumped on the idea. That survey had to be done before planning permission could be given to the builders.

Many councils do not like new estates being built in their town but cannot legally stop them.

The council were quite pleased to do the survey. This gave them a possible reason to say no. They felt that the town had too many new houses anyway. They thought there may be, after all, protected plants as well as animals there. Something like plants called ladies slipper or fen orchid could be looked for. They agreed that an environmental survey should be done. This might take a few weeks to organise.

This gave them, and the cats, a bit of breathing space at least. Jeffrey asked; was it possible to persuade an actual endangered species to move in before the survey was done?

Simba was dispatched to do a reckkie to see what was there. He could not find anything, but something may have been hiding or just came out at night. It was decided that they would have to find an endangered species and persuade them to move in before the council checked.

Obviously, cats cannot dig and replant plants easily. They had to try to put the idea of doing that into their human's heads. This was done without any confidence that they would manage it, but it was worth a try. In the end it did not come to that though.

The next task was to try and get an animal protected species to actually move in. In the short term at least. Dormice would naturally avoid cats at all costs. They would be a no no.

They must try communicating with bats and persuading some of them to move into their patch. There was a tumble down, but brick built shed on the field. This might do for a bat home. It was a possibility, but a tricky one. Did anyone know of any nearby badgers?

They put an emergency call over the cat-o-net. This is a bit like the internet but is a country wide cat communication system. The other cats agreed that badgers were a bad idea. They tend to be surly and obstinate. Probably not prepared to make a major sett (badger home) change and move into unknown territory. They had no interest in helping out a few cats, they had their own little ones to think of.

Bats, now surprisingly that was very easy. A cat in the next county had heard of a split in a roost. A roost is lots of families of bats living together. This particular roost had got too big. More space was needed, and a breakaway group was interested in new territory. The boarded up brick shed with a cellar, on the Close fields, sounded interesting to them. They agreed to check it out.

SW

From his perch on the old BT box/ portal at dusk, a few days later, Jeffrey noticed a number of bats circling round the old brick shed. Then word came back that the move was on. A few days later the rest of the breakaway roost followed and settled in. There was a strict no interference or hunting pact of course. But it was worth it.

The environmental survey found the bats a couple of weeks later. The builders were going to be refused permission to build, for now anyway. They had brought themselves some time.

Then the cats asked themselves what else could they do to hold things up. The next step was a planned individual warfare. There was always the possibility, Patricia said, that the builders would try and get ahead of things. They might start digging up the island

and preparing to put a road through.

This did also need consent, of course, but from a different department. They were counting on one department at the council not sharing information with the other ones. The builders would be sure that they would eventually get the bigger permission anyway.

They could risk starting work on the road anytime. They might start digging and relaying the road for their heavy duty building machines. Once the island was gone it would be gone and portal and peace for ever compromised.

Vigilance was the key. A 24 hour watch and alarm system was set up. Jeffrey had to share his perch with a rota of different cats. The plan was a high pitched yowl was the signal. That would bring them all running at any time of the day or night.

The individual wars started. Any strange cars parked in the Close suddenly found claw marks, damaged soft tops, and mud all over them. Even on dry days. Jeffrey particularly enjoyed ripping almost to shreds a nice fancy soft top on a smart car. It had been left there as someone walked over the field measuring and surveying.

There were complaints of vandalism of course but strangely no one saw anything. Just a few cats playing in the sun.

Jumping on and scratching individuals was another sport. The twins and Simba rather excelled at this. There was a risk of being thrown off, of course, but it was a price worth paying.

Silki specialised in laying in front of cars as they tried to leave. If they picked her up to move her, then against her nature, she would hiss and spit.

Their humans had begun to notice something, although not

realising it was a planned attack. They began to join in a bit. They started putting rubbish through van open windows. Builders' cars were deliberately blocked in.

It was enjoyable to the cats and irritating to the builders. It was realised that it was really not quite enough to stop things though.

Then the day came that they had all been dreading. Notice came to all houses in the Close to move their cars. Diggers were coming in to start work on the road the next week.

The big guns had to be called in. The twins were sent down to go mousing in the portal intergalactic tunnels. Rather than dispatching the negative energies they collected them up. They asked the scariest and the good guys for help.

When Jeffrey saw the first digger round the corner of the close at 6 o'clock one morning he yowled loudly. Every cat came out and took their positions, forming a line across the Close. What was not seen by the humans were the invisible users of the portal that also wanted it saved. They were actually all there as well, giving their support unseen.

The noise also woke up all the humans too. They came to join in, in their pyjamas some of them! It was not a pretty sight!

Bill and Ben thought this was great fun. They started filming and snapping the events. Before long it was going viral on Tik Tok and Instagram, not to mention Facebook. The local and then the national press arrived. The line of cats and their dishevelled owners were on 6.0 o'clock and 7.0 o'clock news. In fact, all the news programmes worldwide.

The builders arrived, rather shame facedly it must be said. They huddled together in the road trying to calm things down and explaining themselves.

 The cat twins released their negative energy captives. The screaming and running as these scary beings played havoc with the group was another Tik Tok hit. I think it even made Sky news. The cat was out of the bag now, so to speak. Their illegal road works were stopped in their tracks. The glare of publicity was too much.

Things went quiet then, the plans were withdrawn, they were safe for now. The portal, and their peace and quiet were secure.

They had to call another conference and release their human links. It has to be said that there was some measure of relief all-round. They could enjoy their lives as cats again. Be cossetted and spoilt, and get some decent napping in.

Jeffrey could go back to his personal car wars and the twins could enjoy their skirmishes with Bill and Ben. Silki could relish the special care offered. Patricia could get plump and lazy to her, and her owners, satisfaction. Simba could concentrate on chasing lady cats. Life at number 44 could go back to its happy chaos. Jameson disappeared for now. No doubt he would return when needed. The Close was at peace. Although the humans did have a big party to celebrate.

Although Jeffrey on his perch at dusk, watching the bats circling around, did feel happy. He also felt something was missing. But then he has always, at heart, been an action cat. He was ready if ever needed again.

JP

SW

A VERY BAD KITTEN

Chapter 1- A naughty new arrival

It had been sometime since the Close had been saved from the evil builders. The cats had enjoyed just being ordinary cats again. Jeffrey had retired from his portal guard duties on the old BT relay box. He preferred these days to be snuggled in his comfy basket in the warmth of his owner's kitchen. His position had been replaced by Simba.

A newcomer to the Close was a small black and white kitten called Bertie. He was the naughtiest cat that the other cats had ever seen. He was not an asset to the Close. In fact he gave the other cats a bad name by his behaviour. Bertie did just not know how to behave.

He had had a very good start to life. Born in a cosy farmhouse kitchen he had two brothers and one sister. He was a very pretty kitten and had been his mother's favourite. He enjoyed love and attention he got from his mum. In fact, he was really spoilt by her.

This all came to a sudden stop one awful day. One day, he was grabbed by strange hands. He was put in a cat carry box and taken away from his cosy home for ever. His new home was in a strange bungalow in a small Close.

There was no warning it was going to happen, and did not even get to say goodbye. He did not even know where he was. Where was mum? Where were Fluffy, Sidney and Mia? He wanted just to go home.

It was a perfectly nice home. There was perfectly nice new people who did love him. But as a spoilt kitten his response to his new home was rage. Who do these people think they are? I am special and deserve better, he thought. He hissed, spat, scratched and bit. He scratched people and furniture.

Mr and Mrs Potts tried to be patient. They were hoping he would settle down. In fact he became worse and worse. There was a particularly nasty scratch given to their baby Charlie. This needed a visit to the doctor, they had had enough.

They sealed the cat flap and moved his basket into the garage.

SW

They fed him twice a day and still had hopes that he would calm down and become the lovely family pet that they really wanted. Bertie had no intention of doing that. Instead, he began a reign of terror.

- He went in though any cat flap he could find and stole food. Either from the cats bowls or anything left out in their owner's kitchens.

- He howled at and fought anyone who came into his garden. He even tried to frighten human visitors off. Some friends just stopped coming.

- He attacked any small children who were walking by his garden. He even tried to jump up onto prams and buggies and bite babies.

- He tried to trip up anyone old and doddery. He succeeded sometimes, although they could never prove it was him. He actually caused minor injuries. Old Mrs Jones broke her wrist and ended up in hospital.

- He tore through dust bins and knocked over food recycling bins. He scattered food and debris over a wide area. The Close was a total mess. The local rats were very pleased with this and encouraged their cousins to come into the area.

- Anyone unsuspecting trying to pet him were in for a shock. He would roll over on his back and when they bent down to tickle his tummy he would do a two claw deep scratch.

It must be said though that none of this made him happy. Other cats shunned him, and he was sad and lonely and sorry for himself, but he could not stop.

Why did nobody love him? Did they not see he was special? Why was there no respect for such a handsome and important cat as he. Did they not know who he was?

The complaints had started to come into the Potts, but they did not know what to do. No one else would adopt him. They were still hoping he would grow out of it. The worst of it was though that he was giving all the Close cats a bad name.

The twins, Brandy and Snap, for instance were cross. Although they were not the most well behaved of cats, they had had a bucket of water thrown over them for something that they did not do. Patricia was never allowed out at all anymore. Kind Silki had tried to befriend him and given up in despair when hissed at. Simba had cuffed him on the ear when he was bad. It had not worked.

The mixed happy cat family at number 44 were fed up at being suspected or blamed for damage. All cats were suffering from the fallout. Cats became to be seen as nuisances by the non cat owners and even the fellow cat owners were fed up. They had started to argue, blaming each other's cats. The usually happy close was becoming not a very nice place to live. People were actually talking about moving.

 Eventually it all came to a head. People's, and cat's patience were at an end. It was when Bertie nearly caused a motorcycle accident which put old Bob's life at risk that things became really serious. He had run out into the road causing Bob to swerve and nearly hit a lamppost.

 It began to be realised that they, the fellow cats, had to do something before the fallout began to affect them badly.

SW

Chapter 2 -The second conference

It was time to call another conference. They assembled in the dusk again on the roundabout near the portal, unseen by the humans. Even Patricia manged to sneak out and join them.

The problem was how to get Bertie to come and face the music? Ever resourceful Jameson collected treats from all his fellow cats and made a trail of them to the green.

Bertie ate them quickly, so no one else would get them, one by one. He reached the middle of the green where the final cat choc was. Then the cats came out of the shadows and made a circle around him. For all his hissing and yowling he was trapped.

He was too full to run away and suddenly began to feel scared. He could feel everyone's eyes on him. He seemed frozen to the spot. Only Jameson stood back, fixing Bertie with his huge scary yellow eyes. Bertie could not move.

Then it began. They circled around him hissing their complaints.

- You tripped my owner over and she broke her wrist.
- You nearly caused old Bob to have a bad accident.
- My owner never lets me out anymore because of you.
- You keep stealing my food.
- We keep getting punished for things we did not do.

- I was blamed and punished for a bad scratch on my owners toddler.

- Rats and rubbish are everywhere.

- People are turning against cats.

- Our quiet lives are being spoilt because of your actions.

They spun faster and faster. They hissed louder and louder. Bertie tumbled over and over, round and round. Then suddenly they were gone. He slunk back to his garage basket exhausted. He was frightened and angry at the same time.

He curled up tight in a ball and fell into a deep sleep. He did not see Jameson standing over him shaking his head sadly. He did not feel anything as Jameson gently but firmly put two huge paws on his head and muttered something important.

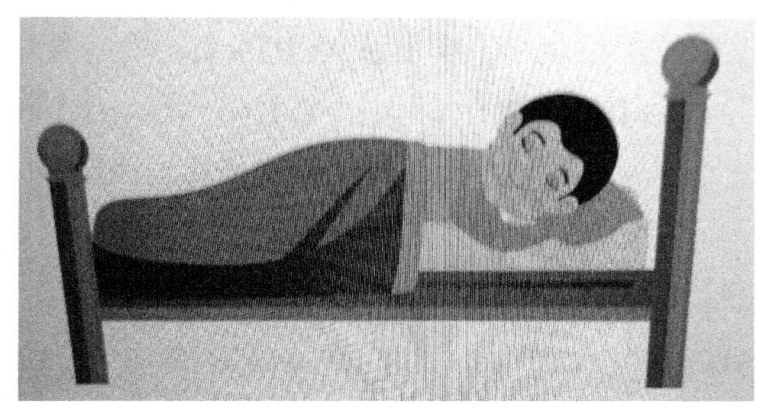

JP

Chapter 3- Master Bertram

He woke up much later with a start. He was totally confused. Where was he? Where was his basket? Why did he seem to be no longer a cat? He had hands not paws. He was sleeping in a huge comfy bed in a large old-fashioned bed room. There was fancy furniture everywhere. There was a cheerful fire in the grate. A large imposing man came in and opened the long heavy damask curtains. Good morning, Master Bertram, the man said. What would you like for breakfast today?

Then he began to remember. He was not a cat at all. He was Bertram Coutts- Melksham. The youngest child, but only son of the vast Coutts- Melksham estate. He would become Viscount Coutts when his father died and he was the heir to everything. That meant he would have all the money and houses. Even now he had loads of servants running round catering for his every whim.

Was the cat thing just a dream? He hoped so because it had not been a pleasant experience. No one had realised how important and special he was.

His parents had gone to London for something called "The Season". This meant lots of fun for everyone apparently. Parties, dances and lots of eating. It was hoped that his sisters would find good rich husbands. The certainly had spent months buying new clothes and wondering who may be available for them to catch.

For reasons he could not explain they had not taken him this year. As he was only 11 they usually left him in the care of his governess in the London house. This worked out quite well usually as she indulged him and took him out to see the sights. She had suddenly left this year, muttering enough is enough.

He had been left in the care of Johnson the butler, who ran the house. Also Mellors the housekeeper, who actually was supposed to look after him. This year he was on his own with the servants.

He was not unhappy about this. He did not like his sisters, and they certainly did not like him.

He thought it was because, as a boy, he was most important. The truth was though they disliked him because he was a horrible brat. He was spoilt and unpleasant to everyone. He also had endless fun bossing the servants about. They were afraid to stand up to him for fear of losing their jobs.

It had begun to dawn on him after a couple of weeks of this, though, that he was lonely. Although they generally tried to avoid him, his sisters were some company. His old nanny who had adored him unconditionally had retired last year and moved to Devon to live with her sister.

The servants also did not like him. They dare not be anything but polite to him but never went beyond that. No one offered to take him out anywhere and he had no invitations from boys of his own age.

Any invitations he asked Johnson to issue to nearby children were also turned down. This was always with a good excuse. But he had slowly begun to realise that no one, however important and special he assumed he was, wanted to spend any time with him.

His breakfast came on a silver tray. Just what he had ordered, but it was not to his liking when it came. A tired looking girl of his own age, Nan, carried it in and placed it carefully on a special table which swung over the bed.

She looked up and half smiled at him. For a moment he thought, she looks nice, perhaps she will be friendly although she is only a servant. For the first time he had seen her as a fellow human being. Then he could not help himself. He threw the breakfast tray onto the floor. Get me a better one he shouted. Those eggs were too runny you idiot.

He turned his face to the wall. He did not see the tears running down her face, perhaps if he had things might have been different, his whole life, not just that moment.

Johnson just stood there frowning. He sent Nan away and pulled a bell for the cleaner to come and clear the mess up. When Bertram turned around to see what was happening, Johnson stood in front of the bed.

He did not allow himself to show anger but sternly looked him straight into his eyes. Johnson's eyes seemed to have turned into glaring yellow cats eyes that Bertram recognised. He could not move. Jameson he stuttered, but there was just Johnson there. I thought that cat stuff was a dream he thought. What is the matter with me?

For a second, he felt a tinge of shame which he quickly pushed down.

Then Johnson/ Jameson spoke. Master Bertram, he said softly but firmly. You have a choice. Either you learn to treat people properly, regardless of their inferior rank and position, or it will impact your life and happiness in the future.

Rage coursed through Bertram's veins. How dare a servant talk to him like that, he thought. He will write to Papa at once and have him sacked. He can talk to people just as he wants to. He is everyone's superior and they will have to just put up with it.

JP

Chapter 4- A revelation

When Nan brought his breakfast the next day there was no smile. She scurried away. He had half thought of saying sorry. Instead, in a temper, he threw the entire breakfast on the floor. To his surprise no one came to clear it up. No one brought him another one. No one came to sort his clothes out and get him up. He was alone all day.

He rang and rang on the bell, and no one answered. When he finally fell to sleep that evening, he had a terrible dream. He was grown up and all alone. He was the Viscount and in charge of everything and had lots of money. But he was sad and lonely.

His sisters had married and gone. They did not include him in their lives. His mother had moved to the South of France, mostly to get away from him he realised. He had no wife. He had no friends. His servants avoided him. He was depressed.

Money, privilege and thinking that you are better and more special than everyone else sounds nice. It does not buy you happiness. He realised that too late. You have to be a nice person and treat other people kindly and fairly, even servants.

The following day, all seemed to be back to normal. His breakfast came. He said thank you to Nan. She half smiled. Johnson looked approvingly at him. I can do this, he thought, I want a happy life.

Unfortunately, of course. he could not keep it up. The temptation to throw his weight around and have massive tantrums if he did not get his own way were too much. The breakfast went on the floor again!

The next thing he knew he felt a paw on his shoulders. He was back in his basket in the garage and Jameson was standing over him. What happened? he asked. You have been given another chance, said Jameson. You messed up your old life as Bertram. He did not learn, but you can if you do the right thing. You are not special in this life you are just a farm kitten.

Remember how you got it wrong last time. You can still turn it around, but you will have to make amends. You can become special, but it will take work.

Bertie did not want a sad lonely life again. He tried then to behave as well as he could. Jameson helped and guided him. He was nice and kind to everyone. He tried to make up for his bad behaviour. This was both to cats and humans, especially those he had harmed.

After a while Jameson called another conference. Bertie said how sorry he was for his behaviour to all the cats. They agreed, in the spirit of Close harmony, to give him another chance. His owners were thrilled with the reformed Bertie and welcomed him back into the house. The better he behaved the more they spoilt him. This time it did not go to his head.

The funny thing was that after a while, once peace had been restored, Jameson seemed to disappear. When the other cats thought about it, no one was ever sure that they had ever known where he had lived. He had just appeared and helped when needed.

The other funny thing was, that when he became a full grown cat, it was Bertie that mostly took over the guarding of the portal and the protection of the Close. He became the wisest of cats. In this life he had earnt his specialness. He never made the same mistakes again.

JP

BOB THE INTERGALACTIC CARAVAN CAT

Chapter1- Imminent danger

Far far away on a large green planet on the other side of the Galaxy a special meeting was going on. The planet was called Dron. On it was the headquarters of something called *The Galactic Council*. The members of the

Council came from all the advanced planets with people on them. They were among the most powerful and clever beings in the Galaxy. They acted as sort of overall government of the inhabited worlds in the galaxy

From Dron they kept a careful eye on all the planets and civilisations on their patch. Their job was not to interfere with them, just to keep watch. They did try to stop any planet wide catastrophes that could cause danger to other worlds. They also usually tried to stop the people living there from destroying their own planets.

A lot of planets with people on them, did not know they were there. Especially those that thought even the idea of aliens and other worlds was utter rubbish! Though this did not stop the Galactic council helping and protecting them when absolutely necessary.

At this particular meeting the topic was planet Earth. Something really bad was going on there. Total environmental disaster was starting to happen. There was pollution everywhere. Trees and crops were dying; rivers were not clean anymore. It was not a good situation. Things could still be rescued though, if things were not made any worse.

Jim, the one person who had an invention that could stop the problem was in danger. He was being hunted by a ruthless gang. The gang were working for other people who liked the way things were.

They wanted to make more money from their own product, even though it resulted in environmental damage. They simply did not care. They thought money was more important than saving the planet.

They saw Jim as the enemy and needed to stop him and his invention. They would do whatever it took, even if it meant getting permanently getting rid of him.

Jim had ended up hiding in a caravan site in a small town. He had no idea what to do next. The Galactic Council had to help him. It was the only way to save him, and probably Earth!

The Council president Mockbar, an imposing 8 foot purple round being, made a decision.

We will have to send our best man to protect him. he said. We will try to buy him time until everyone else notices what is going on and helps him. We do have other agents there working behind the scenes in disguise; they just need a bit longer.

He glanced around the council table. There were many good candidates who could protect Jim. Some were old and wise warriors. Some were known for their diplomatic skills. Some just were well not really there. Just beings made out of energy, hardly solid at all.

His gaze landed on Xorob. He was solid, clever and brave. and had been a good fighter. More usefully, his race could shapeshift. That meant they could change into what shape or being they wanted to. At the moment he was a tall thin being with two heads. Both nodded, he accepted the job.

He was looking forward to the challenge. It was decided he would travel down the energy wormholes to Earth. He would go to the portal which was nearest to the caravan site that Jim was hiding in. The portal was in somewhere called Norman Close. Brisport. in the South of England. The caravan site was just a short walk away.

The problem of what shape of being to become was easily solved by a little research. The most useful thing was to shape-shift into a large but nondescript tabby cat.

He would say that his name was Bob. Cats were special, clever and resourceful animals. People did not always notice them. He would be both anonymous and powerful.

On his flea collar, which some cats wore, he could hide a button for an invisibility cloak. He could also carry a hidden communication device. Then, if necessary, he could link in with other Galactic Council agents for extra help.

There was also a chance that there were other cats on the site where Jim was hiding. They might be useful for spying or distracting purpose. He just had to keep Jim safe for the six months it would take to get his invention officially registered.

Something called a patent was needed. Once this was done then everyone would know about it, and it could not be stopped. Jim's life would be no longer in danger. Earth could be saved. How hard could that be? The mission was to protect Jim without him noticing.

Jim had been really proud of himself when he had worked out a solution to a difficult environmental problem. He had his own company that made things that could help save nature. He thought everyone would be pleased. His invention meant a lot of the damage already done to the environment, could be reversed. To his surprise this was not true. Some businessmen hated it.

He was shocked and disappointed when he realised that this was because they were making so much money from things that were doing the damage. They did not want to stop. They wanted in fact to stop him!

One man even offered to buy his company. Luckily Jim worked out that they just wanted to buy his invention to then just lock it away.

Shortly after he said no, strange things started happening. Clients that he had had for years said they could no longer use him and would not say why. They had obviously been got to and threatened. His company was suddenly in trouble. His flat was burgled and his computers stolen. He often felt he was being followed by strange men. He almost convinced himself that he was imagining it all when he had to jump out of the way when a fast car almost hit him.

He realised he had to hide, or they may well kidnap to even kill him! The official patent registration for his invention would take six months. Only then he would be safe! His invention could not be stopped or disappeared. But where could he go, and how to remain hidden?

He had been watching too many spy films on Nexflix lately, but they had given him an idea. He took as much cash out of his account as he could, so he could vanish. If you paid cash for everything you could not be traced through your bank account. It would be easier to run and hide.

Then he brought an old banger car for cash and stopped off at charity shop for old scruffy clothes. Some hair dye and a pay as you go mobile phone followed.

He locked his flat, put his smart car in his garage. Then he packed a few things then fled out of London. He did not tell anyone what he was doing. Not even his mum and dad knew. He drove and drove in despair for hours.

He stopped driving when he saw a scruffy caravan site on the edge of a small town in Somerset. He pulled in, enquired for vacancies, and paid cash for 6 months rent on a rather sad small caravan. No questions asked. He looked rather shady with his unkempt dyed hair and the start of a beard, not like a successful businessman at all. But then that was rather the point.

Simba had looked slightly puzzled. A strange shape emerged from the portal he was guarding in the Close. It immediately changed itself into a large cat. He seemed to be pleasant enough, no bad vibes, so he did not worry. No need to alert anybody. He did think it odd when this cat asked for directions to the local caravan park in a slightly strange cat accent. But he soon returned to his doze and dreams of chasing field mice which he had been really enjoying. He thought no more about it.

Jim enjoyed no one knowing him for a few days. The other caravan users did not like the look of him and did not speak to him. This did suit him at first. But when he had calmed down from the immediate danger, he realised that he was bored. He still felt a little scared. How was he going to hide here for six months? He was lonely, that is until a rather large but strange cat came to call.

SW

Chapter 2- Bob's arrival

How did the Galactic council know where Jim was? Normally they only take a general view of a planet, its trends and disasters and major changes. They do of course have agents or spies passing as earthlings. They are there generally keeping an eye on things. This is especially when things on a planet seem to be getting dangerous.

They are instructed to look, report back but never (well hardly ever) directly intervene. This was though, a special and urgent case. They had identified what was going on and were secretly watching and trying to protect Jim.

There was a Galactic Council agent pretending to be a road sweeper, who had been following and keeping an eye on Jim. He was lurking outside the old car lot when Jim was buying his car. He managed to stick an advance tracker under Jim's new car. This happened when Jim was inside the building completing the paperwork.

Jim had given them a false name, of course. Hopefully the people that were hunting Jim were not watching him now and had not put their own tracker on. The agent did try and check without being noticed and did not see one though, so all good.

The Council, having tracked Jim's car to Brisport roughly knew where to send Xorob. But he had to find the exact caravan and begin his work. This proved surprisingly easy as the car was actually parked outside a small tatty caravan. Rookie mistake actually…making it easy for anyone to find you like, that is silly. He should have hidden the car at least.

Not particularly a cat lover, Jim was surprisingly pleased to see the tabby. Especially when he made it clear that he intended to move in. Must have belonged to the last person. he thought. Now he is homeless like me. The name Bob came into his mind and the two settled in together.

There was a particular problem though. Bob looked like a cat but actually did not know how to behave like one. Luckily, before this became obvious and drew attention to them both, a large ginger cat strolled over. He also was not exactly who and what he seemed to be.

Who and what are you? Jameson said to Bob. You are certainly not a cat. What are you doing here? Recognising a fellow *off- worlder,* Bob took a chance.

Any signal back to Dron checking if Jameson was actually another agent could be intercepted by the bad guys. This would give the game away for Jim, So Bob used his instincts and asked for his help. He did wonder afterwards whether Jameson was actually expecting him, which of course he was. Who are you yourself? said Bob. My cat name is Jameson, he replied, Happy to help. Galactic Council protection duty top secret. Meet me here at dawn and I will give you a crash course in cattery.

So Bob, was taught the basic skills of being a cat, these included: -

-Enthusiastically demanding and lapping up bowls of milk. It is filthy stuff, but you get used to it.

-Napping on comfy surfaces at all times of the day. Find a good observation point and you can keep one eye open. You can see anyone coming without appearing to look.

-Prowling round for mice or voles. You do not have to catch or eat them, just put on a show of stalking and chasing. Gives you a chance to see where the land lies. Entrances and exits and good hiding places etc. etc

-Meowing for food whether you are hungry or not. I would be careful about joining in any after dark howling that might give you away. It is a complex message exchanging language.

- Stretching and winding yourself around people's legs. It can be a useful weapon. If you are feeling playful you can try and trip them up. Sitting on laps and letting them pet you is expected. Just growl if you have had enough.

- House cats have to chase balls of wool and play with cat toys. I doubt you will need that though.

Bob had to practice meowing and had to adjust his vocal cords to do so.

 But Jameson gave him the all clear eventually before going on his way. The encounter had however, given Bob an idea. In the fellow cats around, he may actually have an army. Now he could pass for a cat, they might actually communicate with him.

This was actually easier said than done. As Jameson had said, there are cats and cats. Some, like himself, are plugged into the International Cat- O -Net and work for the good of all beings (especially cats). Others do their wormhole job when pretending to nap. Some just want to be plain cats. Just bothering about where their next meal or mouse is coming from.

There are however a couple of likely candidates, he thought. I will have a word with them and ask them to keep a look out for strangers. Any sudden howls will be a warning.

SW

Chapter 3- protection duty

Sure enough within a couple of weeks there were definitely more people walking about the site. It could have been coincidence of course but it felt unsettling.

With all the road cameras and CCTV it is relatively easy to track someone. Jim had probably given himself away at somewhere like a petrol station, Bob thought. The gang may have by now tracked him to somewhere in Somerset.

Luckily, they did not know exactly where he was. If they had his new car number plate, they could more easily find him. Of if he switched his original mobile phone on, or talked to any of his family, he would give the game away! Switching his computer on and using WIFI might also be dodgy.

Bob first had to get rid of Jim's mobile phone. Phones can send out location information without necessarily being switched on. It was easy enough to knock the phone down onto the floor somewhere Jim would stand on it and break it.

The computer was only switched on via site WiFi for the news. Childs play to nudge a cup of tea over the keyboard as Jim went past. Using his paws to muddy up the car numberplate had also been worth doing.

The first warning howls came a week or so afterwards. He had found a good hiding place in the woods near the site. Bob grabbed Jim's cigarettes in his mouth and ran into the woods with Jim chasing after him. He manged to keep him out of his caravan until the danger passed. The telling off was worth it!

The second set of warning howls came shortly afterwards. Jameson had talked to some of the local cats. They agreed to do at bit of annoying mobbing and hissing.

This did send the next intruder away. He was frightened of cats. Bob knew that this would only be the start of it. He would have to take more drastic measures if he was going to succeed in his mission of protecting Jim.

He did, however, have three secret weapons.

First, on his flea collar he had the invisibility cloak button. Also, as a last resort, a communications button.

Secondly, he could call in human re-enforcements. This would involve activating his communication button. Might do more harm than good if someone else intercepts the signal. But might be worth the risk.

Thirdly, he was, after all, a warrior with years of experience. Also, he had Jameson who had been sent to help him after all!

The third lot of warning howls came a week later. Luckily Jim was actually out shopping. Bob changed himself into a human shape totally unlike Jim. He answered the knock on the door and showed himself not to be Jim. He became someone large and menacing looking. The intruders apologised and they went away.

The fourth time he heard them coming and sat on Jim's knee and pressed the invisibility button on his flea collar. This did cloak them for 15 minutes or so. Although when Jim picked up his cup of tea it was a scary moment as his hand came outside the cloak range. He was puzzled but relieved that the intruders did not seem to notice him.

These were only short-term solutions; he knew that time was running out. The enemy appeared to be homing in on him; they knew he was there somewhere. There was only a couple of weeks left though, and he would be safe.

JP

Chapter 4 -The rescue

As if by magic, or telepathy, Jameson turned up again the next day. A cat army would not do it this time; it would have to be human.

If one of the Galactic Council's human agents could be reached, reinforcements could be triggered.

An appeal went out over the Cat-O- Net. The request went straight to the top. The most important cats had human connections which they could activate in dire emergency. The message was sent through, and the alert was given.

Agents began to plan an extraction and protection manoeuvre. These last few weeks were the most dangerous though. The future of Jim and the planet was at stake!

Before this could happen, the worst attack began. Two men burst into the Caravan late at night and tried to take Jim away. They could not believe their eyes when this tatty cat changed his shape into a huge warrior. He tied them both up and carried them back to their car.

He put them into a 24 hour sleep; they were never the same again. Jim just thought he had been dreaming, but Bob knew how serious this was. The bad guys never quite knew what had happened. They could not explain their failure to their shady bosses.

Then at last, a smart blue car with blacked out windows came to the Caravan site. Galactic council human agents picked Jim up and took him to safety. He did not know exactly who they were. They looked human and he knew they were the good guys. His nightmare was over. His invention had been saved. He had been saved. The planet had been saved. He looked to say goodbye to Bob, but Bob was gone.

 Bob and Jameson strolled together back towards the portal." Thanks for your help" said Xorob as de-catted and became himself again. But I will ask you the same question that you asked me. Who are you really and what are you doing here? Jameson smiled a cat smile.

I have quite enjoyed being a cat, he said. I helped solve several problems here and saved the portal while I was waiting for you. But my work here is done for now.

He momentarily shifted into another being. It was done so quickly that Xorob could not really tell what it was. They both waved at Bertie and disappeared down through the portal under the old BT relay box together. Then they returned to their home planets through the wormholes. Who and what was he really? Where was home? Ahh, said Jameson, well that is another story.

The Galactic council looked down on Earth with some satisfaction. Nature was recovering, trees were growing again, and pollution was getting a lot better. Earth was saved from total environmental disaster. Their job was done. They could turn their attention to other planets that needed their help now. Perhaps with the help of Bob and Jameson in future, whoever they really are!

163

Printed in Dunstable, United Kingdom